EXTREME!

UFOs
and Aliens

Investigating Extraterrestrial Visitors

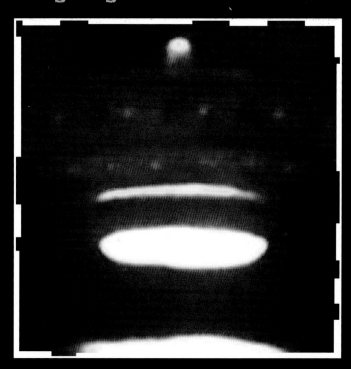

Produced for A & C Black by

MONKEY PUZZLE MEDIA LTD

Monkey Puzzle Media Ltd
Little Manor Farm, Brundish,
Woodbridge, Suffolk IP13 8BL, UK

Published by A & C Black Publishers Limited
36 Soho Square, London W1D 3QY

First published 2009

ISBN 978-1-4081-1475-9 (hardback)
ISBN 978-1-4081-1995-2 (paperback)

The right of Paul Mason to be identified as the
author of this Work has been asserted by him in
accordance with the Copyright, Designs and
Patents Act 1988.

A CIP catalogue record for this book is available
from the British Library.

Editor: Susie Brooks
Design: Mayer Media Ltd
Picture research: Lynda Lines
Series consultants: Jane Turner and James de Winter

This book is produced using paper that is made
from wood grown in managed, sustainable forests.
It is natural, renewable and recyclable. The logging
and manufacturing processes conform to the
environmental regulations of the country of origin.

Printed in Singapore by Tien Wah Press (Pte.) Ltd

Picture acknowledgements
Alamy p. 10–11 (David Hosking); Corbis pp. 6 (Gerd
Ludwig), 7 (Bettmann); Getty Images p. 15 (AFP);
Mary Evans Picture Library pp. 10, 14; MPM Images
pp. 1, 4, 22–23, 24, 25 left and right, 26, 28 top;
NASA pp. 12, 13, 28–29; Scince Photo Library p.
16 (Peter Menzel); Topfoto.co.uk pp. 5 (Fortean),
8 (The Granger Collection), 8–9 (Fortean), 17
(Fortean), 18 (Fortean), 19 (Fortean), 20 (Fortean),
21 (Fortean), 27 (Fortean). The artwork on p. 22 is
by Tim Mayer.

The front cover shows an artist's impression of an
alien (Getty Images/Antonio M Rosario).

Every effort has been made to contact copyright
holders of material reproduced in this book. Any
omissions will be rectified in subsequent printings if
notice is given to the publishers.

CONTENTS

Abbreviations m stands for metres • **ft** stands for feet • **°C** stands for degrees Centigrade •
°F stands for degrees Farenheit

UFO fever!

Imagine you're driving along a lonely road, late at night. Suddenly, the engine stops and the lights go out. A dark shape looms overhead. You **MIGHT** be about to meet a UFO!

UFO stands for "unidentified flying object". In theory, anything that flies can be a UFO, if the person looking at it doesn't know what it is. But when most people hear the word UFO, they think of just one thing – visitors from outer space.

UFOlogists claim that aliens have been visiting Earth for thousands of years. Here are a few examples:
- A "round shield" seen in the skies above Arpi, Italy, in 216 BC.
- In 170 BC at Lanupim, near Rome, a whole fleet of ships seen in the air.
- Ancient cave paintings that show images similar to modern diagrams of UFOs.

*People once thought the mysterious **Nazca Lines** in Peru were made by alien vehicles.*

Alien landing strips

During the 1970s, some people thought (wrongly) that the Nazca Lines of Peru were alien landing strips. It seemed that aliens had been visiting Earth for thousands of years!

UFOlogists people who study UFOs

4

Nazca Lines designs in the ground made by the ancient Nazca people of Peru

5

Investigating UFOs

Could beings from other planets really be visiting Earth? There are certainly plenty of people who fake **UFO** sightings and alien encounters. But in among the fakes, are there some *real* UFOs?

Alien energy

UFOs are thought to leave behind materials that are **radioactive**. Scientists use a device called a Geiger counter to test for radiation.

A scientist tests the air for traces of energy – perhaps they were left behind by a UFO!

UFOlogists ask a variety of questions to help them decide whether sightings are real or not:

- Do all the **witnesses** say the same thing? If there is only one witness, does that person seem trustworthy?
- Are there any clues, such as wreckage or chemical **traces**, that show a UFO has been there?
- Do any photos look real? Examining photos can reveal a lot of fakes!

radioactive giving off a type of energy called radiation

No one else is around.

"UFOs" were added to the sky later.

Spectators pose as though looking at the UFOs.

This UFO photo from Sicily in Italy was taken in 1954 — but it turned out to be a fake.

witness a person who sees something   **traces** things left behind

The coming of the saucers

On 24 June 1947, American pilot Kenneth Arnold spotted a group of objects he called "flying saucers". Apparently they were whizzing through the sky at an impossible speed! What were these incredible craft?

Could the UFOs have been XB-35 planes, like this one?

Experimental aircraft

Some investigators thought that Arnold might have seen an experimental XB-35 plane. The trouble was, there was only one of these – and at the time, it couldn't fly!

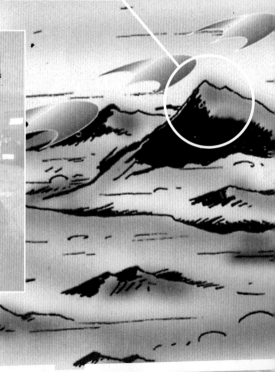

Mount Rainier

USSR the country that later became Russia

At first, Arnold mistook the flying objects for geese — but then he worked out that they were travelling at an amazing 1,900 kilometres per hour (1,180 miles per hour)! Other explanations were soon put forward:

1) The **USSR**, America's rival, had developed an amazingly fast aeroplane.
2) America had secretly developed its own fast plane.
3) The craft had not been made on Earth at all — but had come from outer space!

The last explanation was the most popular. Within days, the first UFO craze had begun.

Kenneth Arnold spotted nine "UFOs" while flying near Mt Rainier, USA.

Arnold saw the UFOs pass Mt Rainier, then pass another mountain 1 minute, 42 seconds later.

Arnold worked out the UFOs' speed by dividing the distance they travelled by the time it took.

Was Arnold wrong?

Investigators today think that Arnold got his speed sums wrong. The flying objects were really much closer to Arnold than he thought — which meant the distance they had flown was much less.

A signed copy of Kenneth Arnold's book The Flying Saucer as I Saw It.

What Arnold saw

The day after the sighting, Arnold described the UFOs he had seen. They were:

- A string of objects flying along, dipping up and down like a saucer skipping on water.
- Only clearly seen when the Sun shone on them, with black wingtips.
- Flying at high **altitude**.

All these things match the way pelicans fly along in groups.

altitude height above sea level

Is it a bird?

Though many people thought they were visitors from outer space, there is a much simpler explanation for what Arnold saw. They were pelicans! Flights of American white pelicans are often seen in the area. They fly at high altitude, have black wingtips, and fly in a rising-and-falling line.

American white pelicans are similar in shape and colouring to Arnold's "UFOs".

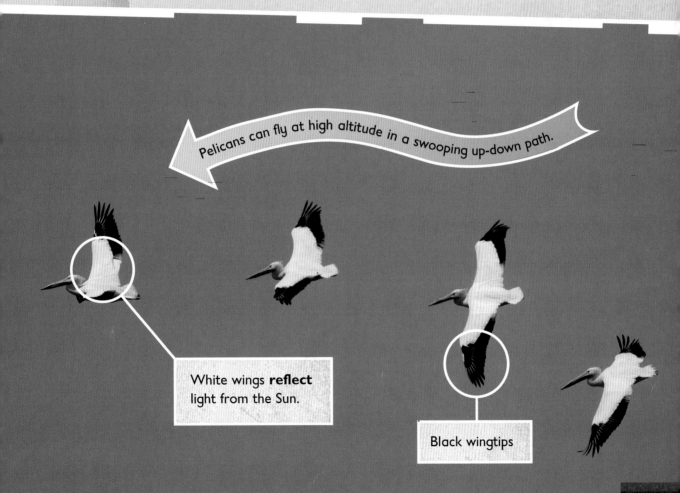

Pelicans can fly at high altitude in a swooping up-down path.

White wings **reflect** light from the Sun.

Black wingtips

reflect to bounce back rays of light

UFOs and astronauts

Many people dream of what it would be like to travel into space. But imagine being up in your spacecraft – and suddenly realizing you're not alone!

There are many stories about astronauts seeing UFOs while up in space. But have any of them turned out to be true?

Rumour: 1962, John Glenn saw three objects overtake his spacecraft.

Explanation: He did. They were ice crystals that had formed on the spacecraft's sides, then been shaken off.

Rumour: March 1965, Russian astronauts saw a cylindrical object circling around the Earth.

Explanation: They did – and they also realized it was a **satellite**, put there by humans.

Rumour: November 1966, Jim Lovell and Buzz Aldrin saw a line of FOUR UFOs.

Explanation: They weren't unidentified – they were four bags of rubbish the astronauts had just ejected!

John Glenn was the first American to fly a spacecraft around the Earth. But what did he see up there?

satellite a machine that is sent into space to collect and send back information

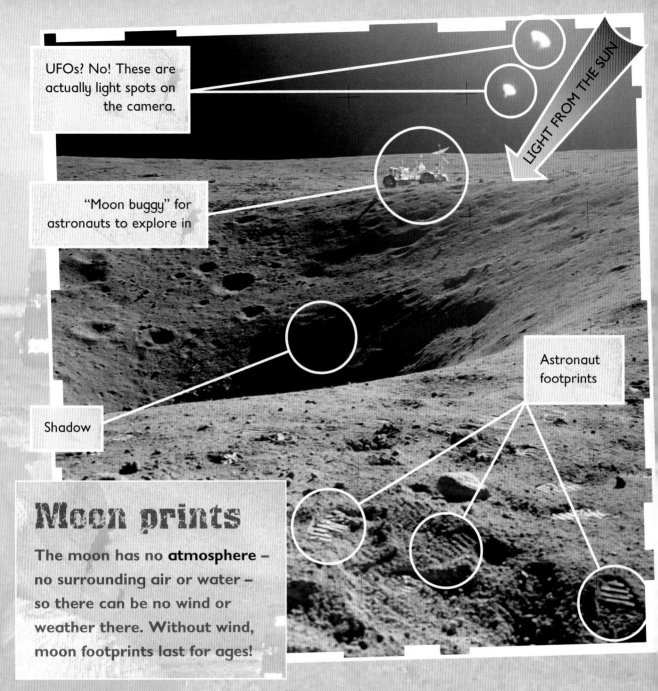

UFOs? No! These are actually light spots on the camera.

LIGHT FROM THE SUN

"Moon buggy" for astronauts to explore in

Astronaut footprints

Shadow

Moon prints

The moon has no **atmosphere** – no surrounding air or water – so there can be no wind or weather there. Without wind, moon footprints last for ages!

People claimed that there were UFOs in this photo of the moon's surface, taken in 1972.

atmosphere the layer of gases that surrounds a planet like Earth

Incident at Roswell

In July 1947, a series of mysterious events began at Roswell, USA, that still cause arguments today. Did a UFO crash-land there? And were alien bodies recovered from the wreckage – or even living aliens?

"AIR FORCE CAPTURES FLYING SAUCER" shouted the headline in the local paper. The story said that a local **rancher** had discovered the wreckage of a crashed UFO near Roswell, New Mexico, USA. The wreckage had various strange properties, and seemed to be made of materials that no one had seen before.

An artist's impression shows the crashed UFO near Roswell.

Alien invasion

The UFO crash at Roswell, coming soon after the Arnold flying-saucer sightings, made some people fear that an alien invasion was about to begin!

rancher a cattle or sheep farmer

Major Jesse Marcels of the US Air Force holds wreckage from the "UFO" crash site.

The UFO wreckage had several strange features:
- A mysterious metallic cloth that was very light but would not tear.
- Black, plastic-like material that had been melted or burned.
- Lightweight **struts** with weird violet symbols on them.

struts supports

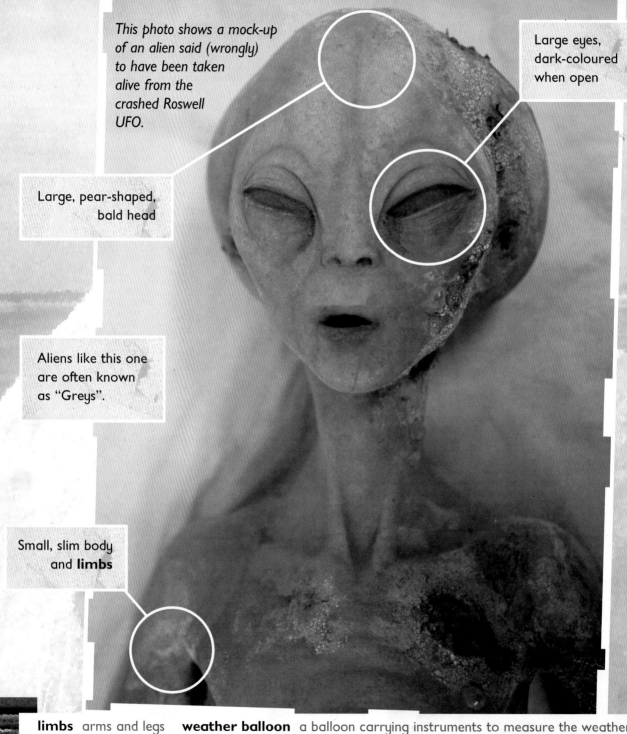

This photo shows a mock-up of an alien said (wrongly) to have been taken alive from the crashed Roswell UFO.

Large eyes, dark-coloured when open

Large, pear-shaped, bald head

Aliens like this one are often known as "Greys".

Small, slim body and **limbs**

limbs arms and legs   **weather balloon** a balloon carrying instruments to measure the weather

Air Force denials

The day after the Roswell UFO story appeared, the US Air Force denied it was true. They said that what had actually crashed was a **weather balloon**.

Supporters of the UFO theory pointed out that the mysterious materials apparently discovered at the site were not used in weather balloons. Rumours grew of a government **cover-up**.

Alien guests

Stories claim that living aliens were taken from the crashed Roswell **UFO**. All the "evidence" of this has turned out to be fake.

A modern photo shows where the Roswell crash happened.

The truth emerges

Many years later, an explanation of what happened at Roswell emerged. The government had been trying a cover-up – of its *own* UFO! The UFO was code-named Project Mogul. It was not a spaceship, but a secret device designed to listen for attacks on the USA. Project Mogul was towed behind a string of weather balloons.

cover-up an attempt to hide the truth

Photographic "evidence"

Over the years, plenty of photos have seemed to prove that UFOs really exist. The trouble is, you don't have to look very hard to see that the photos are fakes!

Hoaxers traditionally used three main methods of faking UFO photos:

1) Joining two photos together, then re-photographing the joined bits to make a single picture.
2) Adding an object – a Frisbee or a button, for example – to a photo so it looks like a UFO.
3) Taking two photos on one piece of film, so that both images blend together when a photo is printed from the film. This makes it possible to "put" a fake UFO in the sky.

FAKE! In this photo from Australia in 1954, the UFO looks much sharper than the sheep – even though it is further away.

hoaxer someone who tricks people

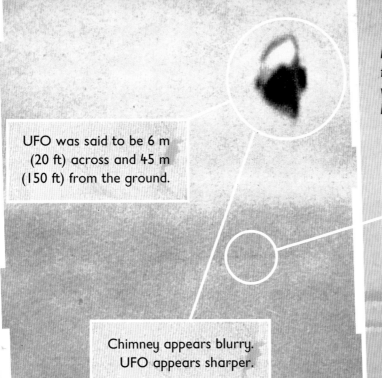

FAKE! When this 1962 photo from Melbourne, Australia was examined, experts soon knew it was a *fraud*.

UFO was said to be 6 m (20 ft) across and 45 m (150 ft) from the ground.

Up close, a jagged line through the clouds shows that two photos have been joined.

Chimney appears blurry. UFO appears sharper.

How to spot a fake

- If two photos have been joined, you can usually see the join through a magnifying glass.
- The edges of fake objects often look sharper than you'd expect if they were a long way away.

fraud a fake produced to make money

The Avensa Airline hoax

What would it be like to be jetting off on your holidays, only to look out of the plane window and see a flying saucer alongside? A bit scary!

In October 1966, a mysterious photo convinced many people that aliens were taking their holidays on Earth! A pilot for Avensa Airlines had apparently taken the photo. It showed a flying saucer below an aeroplane, with both aircraft casting shadows on the forest below. Could the photo prove that UFOs really existed?

A "UFO" visits Viborg, Denmark in 1974. But does it look more like a cloud to you?

The hoaxer confesses

In 1971, a Venezuelan engineer confessed to faking the Avensa Airlines photo. The UFO was actually... a button!

FAKE! UFO appears too sharp to be large and distant.

REAL? Shadows of the plane and the UFO are both in the right place.

FAKE! UFO's shadow is not as dark as the plane's — even though both are solid objects.

REAL? Both shadows are similarly blurred.

The Avensa Airlines photo apparently shows a UFO flying over the Venezuelan rain forest.

Gulf Breeze

Florida – home to beautiful beaches, the Everglades, Walt Disney World... and, at the small town of Gulf Breeze, one of the world's hottest UFO hotspots!

The first UFO sighting was by a man named Ed Walters in 1987. Soon after, Gulf Breeze became UFO central. There were hundreds of sightings a year, plus reports of attempted kidnappings by aliens.

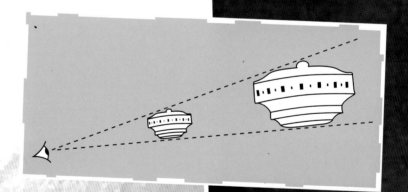

At night-time, it's tricky to tell how far away an object is. A small object nearby and a large object far away look very similar.

At first, the UFOs were mainly red lights in the sky. Then, in 1991, a new kind of UFO began to appear. This looked much more like people imagined an alien craft should be, with windows along the side and a power source glowing underneath.

octagonal eight-sided

This photo was taken by Ed Walters. It shows the UFO that began to appear above Gulf Breeze in September 1991.

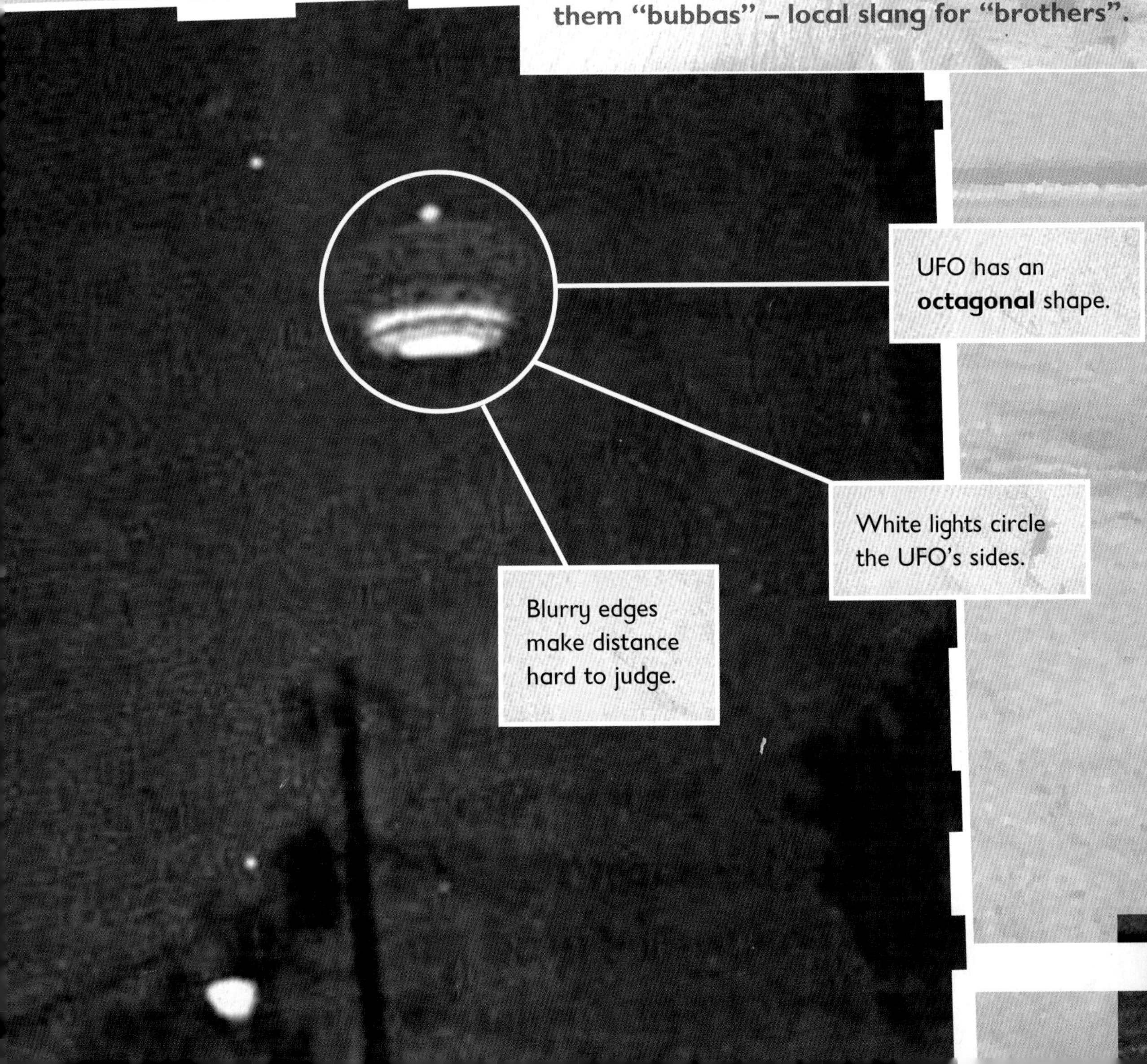

Brothers from outer space

The red-light **UFOs** in Gulf Breeze often appeared in pairs. People began calling them "bubbas" – local slang for "brothers".

UFO has an **octagonal** shape.

White lights circle the UFO's sides.

Blurry edges make distance hard to judge.

Fact or fraud?

Some people began to suggest that Ed Walters was using his UFO sightings to make money. The trouble was, lots of other people had seen the UFOs too. They couldn't all be in on the same fraud.

Two of Ed Walters' UFO photos (left and below) and a photo (right) showing the remarkably similar model UFO found in his old house.

Double exposure

Walters is said to have faked his UFO photos using "double exposure" photography. This involves taking two photos on one piece of film. Both images then appear in one picture.

A model explanation

Finally, an explanation seemed to emerge:

- In a house where Walters had once lived, a model of a UFO was discovered. The model was roughly 25 centimetres (10 inches) across, and wrapped up in paper. The model UFO looked just like the ones in many of Ed Walters' photos.
- A local teenager came forward and admitted helping Ed and his son to fake the photos.

It seemed clear that the pictures had been faked. The witnesses had not seen a real UFO – just a model.

Incident at Rendlesham

In the middle of a cold December night, sentries at an Air Force base in Rendlesham Forest, England saw strange lights in the woods. It was the start of one of England's most famous UFO stories.

Three men headed into the forest to investigate the lights. They came back saying that they had seen a UFO. It was either hovering above the ground or resting on thin legs.

The next night, red and blue lights were seen in the forest. As investigators approached, the lights disappeared. It later turned out that a security officer had faked them, using the flashing lights on his car!

Do these lights in Rendlesham Forest look like UFOs to you?

sentries people, usually soldiers, on guard

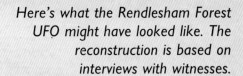

Here's what the Rendlesham Forest UFO might have looked like. The reconstruction is based on interviews with witnesses.

No explanation

The strange events on the first night in Rendlesham Forest have never been explained. BUT, no one has ever come up with any evidence that they were caused by a UFO.

3 m (10 ft) across

2 m (6.5 ft) high

Three dents were found in the ground where the UFO had been.

Dents contained radioactive materials, suggesting something unusual.

27

Life on Mars?

Mars is clearly visible from Earth. For centuries, people wondered if there could be life there too — and if so, was it friendly?

This enlargement seems to show an alien — or is it just a rock?

Huge dust storms sometimes cover the planet.

probe an exploratory vehicle   **barren** unable to grow plants

In 1898, a book called *The War of the Worlds* appeared. In it, invaders from Mars arrive on Earth, determined to take over the planet. When a radio version of the book was broadcast in 1938, thousands of people thought aliens really had appeared!

Humans have now sent **probes** to Mars. We knew already that there could be no Martians there. The planet is **barren**, with extreme temperatures and a thin atmosphere. But scientists hoped to find out more about Earth's next-door neighbour.

Squashed Martians

Gravity on Earth is three times stronger than on Mars. If Martians existed, our gravity would probably crush them.

This photo of Mars was taken by a probe and beamed back to Earth.

In winter, temperatures drop to -140°C (-220°F).

Mars's atmosphere is too thin for living things to survive.

There's no running water, so nothing to drink.

gravity a force that attracts objects to each other

29

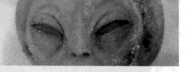

Glossary

altitude height above sea level

atmosphere the layer of gases that surrounds a planet like Earth

barren unable to grow plants

cover-up an attempt to hide the truth.

fraud a fake produced to make money

gravity a force that attracts objects to each other

hoaxer someone who tricks people

limbs arms and legs

Nazca Lines designs in the ground made by the ancient Nazca people of Peru

octagonal eight-sided

probe an exploratory vehicle

radioactive giving off a type of energy called radiation

rancher a cattle or sheep farmer

reflect to bounce back rays of light

satellite a machine that is sent into space to collect and send back information

sentries people, usually soldiers, on guard

struts supports

traces things left behind

UFOlogists people who study UFOs

USSR the country that later became Russia

weather balloon a balloon carrying instruments to measure the weather

witness a person who sees something

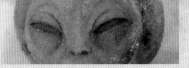

Further information

Books

Investigating UFOs by Paul Mason (Heinemann Library, 2004)
Tells the story of some of the world's most famous UFO cases, and the scientific investigations into what actually happened. Includes the chance to try and solve your own UFO mystery.

The UFO Hunter's Handbook by Caroline Tiger (Puffin Books, 2001)
Great fun, this spoof guidebook tells you lots of information about UFOs and the aliens that drive them. Contains quizzes and diagrams as well.

Alien Encounters: True Life Stories of Aliens, UFOs and Other Extra-terrestrial Phenomena by Rupert Matthews (Arcturus Foulsham, 2008)
Includes details of UFO sightings and encounters with aliens.

UFOs: Are They Real? by David Orme (Ransom Publishing, 2006)
This book starts with a factual section introducing the basics of UFOlogy, which is followed by a gripping fictional story about UFOs.

Magazines

Fortean Times
Fortean Times is inspired by Charles Fort, a writer who in the early 1900s collected information about events that science couldn't explain. The magazine often carries articles about UFOs, as well as other weird phenomena.

Websites

www.forteantimes.com
The website of *Fortean Times* magazine, with plenty of extra features including stories about strange happenings in places you might visit (or live!).

www.ufocasebook.com
This site contains information about every aspect of UFOs and aliens. There's also a collection of UFO photos.

www.ufoevidence.org
Click on "UFO photographs". You can look at the photos either by decade or by geographical location.

Films

The Abyss directed by James Cameron (20th Century Fox, 1989)
Mysterious underwater events turn out to have been caused by curious aliens deep underwater.

The Day the Earth Stood Still directed by Robert Wise (20th Century Fox, 1951)
A friendly UFO appears above Washington, USA, but disaster follows.

Mars Attacks! (Warner Bros, 1996)
Director Tim Burton's parody-tribute to the UFO movies of the 1950s.

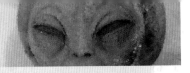

Index